MAKE YOUR OWN

NERF

LAUNCHERS

SCHOLASTIC INC.

ISBN 978-1-338-66323-5

10 9 8 7 6 5 4 3 2 1   21 22 23 24 25

Printed in China   68
First edition 2021

Book design by Jessica Mercado
Written by Kris Hirshmann
Special thanks to the late Dr. Andre Adle from New York University for his
valuable help on this book.

TABLE OF CONTENTS

FIRE AWAY!

Everybody loves NERF blasters! What else gives you the ability to send zippy foam darts flying across the room? Nothing, that's what. That's why here at NERF, we like to say: It's NERF or nothin'!

In this kit, you'll learn how projectiles—like those supercool darts—actually work. You'll even invent your own! Crack open this kit to learn how to make and use object-flinging beasts like catapults, slingshots, and crossbows, along with a bunch of other launchers. Get ready to have a **BLAST**!

IN THIS KIT

PUNCH-OUT CATAPULT AND SLINGSHOT

Punch out the cardboard pieces and assemble them to make a cool catapult and a sweet slingshot.

RUBBER BANDS

You need plenty of rubber bands for the activities in this kit. You got 'em!

AIR-POWERED LAUNCHER

Use this launch pad to blast darts into the air and send them flying.

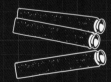

THREE NERF DARTS

Take aim and fire away with these classic darts.

ONE FOAM BALL

More stuff to fire!

SAFETY FIRST

It's fun to send stuff flying, but you need to be safe about it. Follow these rules for responsible blasting.

GATHER everything you need before starting each activity.

CLEAN UP when you're done working. No one likes a slob!

NEVER AIM at people, animals, or breakable objects.

FLING ONLY SOFT THINGS like the foam balls and darts provided, marshmallows, cotton balls, or other light, squishy objects. In other words, stay away from sharp, pointy, or heavy stuff.

ALWAYS FOLLOW THE INSTRUCTIONS EXACTLY. Ask for adult help or do activities outdoors when instructed.

ONLY USE OFFICIAL NERF DARTS for the activities in this kit. Other darts may not meet safety standards.

USE YOUR COMMON SENSE. We know you have some.

SCIENCE IS A BLAST!

When you pick up that awesome NERF blaster and send a dart winging across the room, guess what? The dart is still a dart. But it also has a scientific name. The dart has temporarily become a **PROJECTILE**.

In science lingo, a projectile is any object that moves through space or air and is subject only to gravity and **AIR RESISTANCE** (if any). In other words, if you throw it, pitch it, kick it, blast it, shoot it, or toss it—it's a projectile.

The path of a projectile is called its **TRAJECTORY**. The shape of the trajectory depends partly on whether there is air resistance and partly on the angle at which it is propelled. If a projectile is traveling upward at first, it follows a curved path called a **PARABOLA**. This means it rises at first, then levels off, then begins to descend, until finally it falls to the ground, as if it were going up a hill and then down the hill.

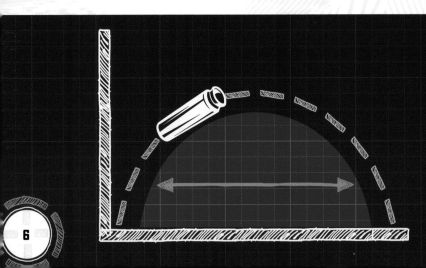

ALL ABOUT GRAVITY

GRAVITY is the main **FORCE** at work on a projectile. Other forces, like air resistance, may have a small effect, but gravity is the main player. If an object creates any forward or upward force of its own (called **THRUST**), it's not a projectile.

NOT A PROJECTILE

X **Floating helium balloon**

X **Car being driven**

X **Tetherball**

X **Cloud**

PROJECTILE

✓ **Dropped lead balloon**

✓ **Car falling off a bridge**

✓ **Tennis ball hit by a racket**

✓ **Hailstone falling from the sky**

FUN WITH PROJECTILES

But enough with the science. Let's focus on the important point: Projectiles are **AWESOME**. It's fun to blast things across the room or your backyard. The bigger the blastoff, the cooler it is—and there are some really major launches in this book. Intrigued? You should be. Let's make some projectiles fly!

COOL CATAPULT

A catapult is a device that launches things via the sudden release of stored energy. Build your very own catapult, and see its amazing launch power in action!

ASSEMBLING THE CATAPULT

1. Punch out the cardboard pieces. There will be twenty-one pieces. There are some extras of the very smallest, most delicate pieces, just in case any break.

2. Assemble the catapult using the pictures as a guide.

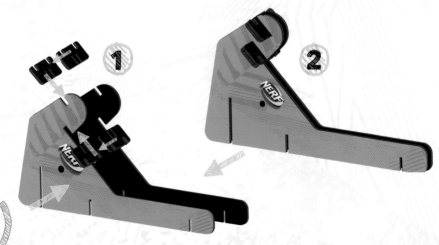

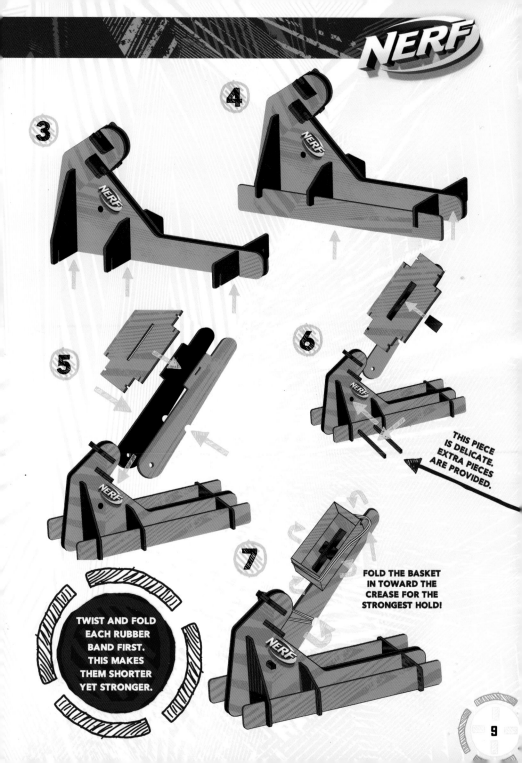

NERF

3

4

5

6

THIS PIECE IS DELICATE. EXTRA PIECES ARE PROVIDED.

7

FOLD THE BASKET IN TOWARD THE CREASE FOR THE STRONGEST HOLD!

TWIST AND FOLD EACH RUBBER BAND FIRST. THIS MAKES THEM SHORTER YET STRONGER.

USING THE CATAPULT

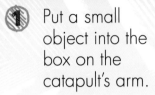

1 Put a small object into the box on the catapult's arm.

2 Push the catapult's arm down all the way, then quickly let it go. Watch the projectile go **FLYING!**

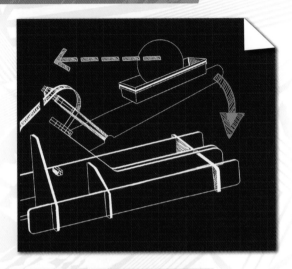

READY, AIM, SCIENCE!

Objects have two types of energy:

POTENTIAL ENERGY is energy that is stored owing to an object's position or arrangement.

KINETIC ENERGY is the energy of an object in motion. When you push down on the catapult's arm, you create tons of potential energy. The rubber band gains potential energy because it is stretched, which builds **TENSION**. The catapult arm and the projectile also have potential energy due to their location on Earth, which has gravity, and height above the ground. All that potential energy turns into kinetic energy as the rubber band, catapult arm, and projectile spring into action!

ANGLE OF ATTACK

In the last activity, you pushed the catapult's arm down all the way to launch your projectile. What do you think would happen if you pushed it down partway? There's only one way to find out!

WHAT YOU NEED

- Assembled catapult
- Projectile of your choice
- Tape measure
- Pen or pencil
- Chart on page 14 of this book

LAUNCH TEST

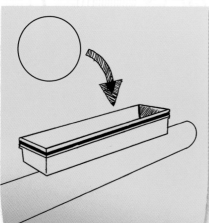

1 Put the projectile into the box on the catapult's arm.

2 Push the arm down all the way, then release it. Watch the projectile fly. Take note of the spot where it lands.

3 Use the tape measure to find the distance between the catapult and the projectile's landing spot. Record the distance in the chart on page 14.

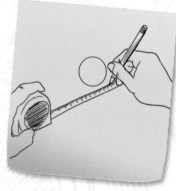

4 Retrieve the projectile and try again, but this time push the arm down about three-quarters of the way before releasing it. Where does the projectile land this time? Measure and record.

5 Repeat two more times, pushing the arm down half of the way and then one-quarter of the way.

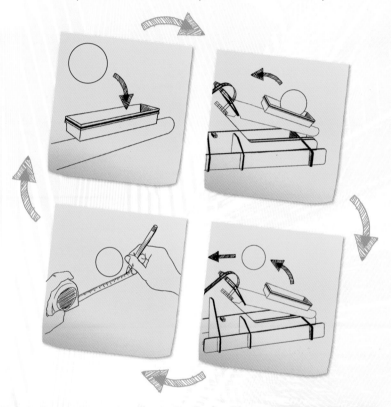

READY, AIM, SCIENCE!

A projectile's travel distance and trajectory depend on two things: the force and the direction of launch. Greater force gives the projectile a greater push, but if the trajectory is a high arc, the projectile may not travel very far forward. You have to experiment to find the combination of perfect push and trajectory for maximum distance.

FLIGHT FACTS

Record your launch data on this page.
(Note: The fractions are approximate. Just do your best.)

DATE:

LOCATION:

PROJECTILE:

When you push the arm down this far:	The projectile flies this far:
One-quarter of the way	
Half of the way	
Three-quarters of the way	
All the way	

Which setting gave you the longest flight?

Which setting gave you the shortest flight?

Why do you think you got the results you did? Explain your thoughts here:

LET IT FLY

You don't need a fancy catapult to launch things across the room. This simple launching arm is quick and easy to make, and it will let you launch small projectiles with ease.

WHAT YOU NEED

- Toilet paper tube
- Rubber band
- Wooden spoon
- Small projectile

MAKE THE LAUNCHER

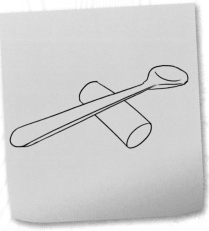

1 Set the wooden spoon across the middle of the toilet paper tube. Half of the spoon should stick out on either side.

Wrap the rubber band around the tube and the spoon twice in an X pattern to hold them together.

Set the contraption on the floor with the spoon end touching the floor and the handle angled upward.

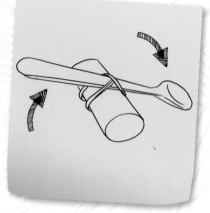

Set your projectile on the spoon.

Slam your hand down on the handle. The spoon rotates up and **POW**—your projectile goes flying!

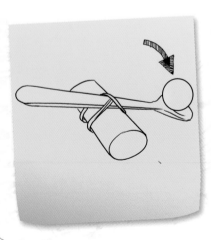

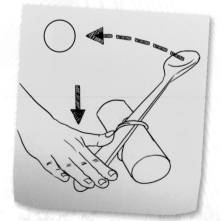

READY, AIM, SCIENCE!

The catapult and your spoon launcher both use force to launch projectiles, but the source of that force's energy is different. The catapult used stored energy from rubber bands. The spoon launcher uses pushing energy from your body. Either way, the result is a rotating arm that swings up and tosses your projectile across the room!

NAPKIN LAUNCHER

If you have an emergency need to launch a small object, this napkin launcher is just the thing. No assembly required!

WHAT **YOU** NEED

- A napkin
- A small projectile

LAUNCH YOUR LUNCH

1 Place the projectile in the center of the napkin.

② Hold two opposite edges of the napkin, one edge in each hand. Bring your hands together so the middle of the napkin sags downward.

③ Quickly yank the edges apart. The napkin straightens out and your projectile blasts upward!

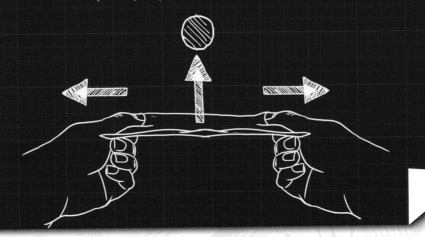

READY, AIM, SCIENCE!

Energy is getting transferred all over the place here. Your body supplies energy when you yank the napkin's edges. This energy goes into the napkin. The napkin transfers the energy to the object. Up it goes!

SWEET SLINGSHOT

It's time to transfer some more energy! This time you'll use your pulling power to load a slingshot and blast a foam ball across the room.

MAKE THE SLINGSHOT

1 Punch out the cardboard pieces. There will be two pieces.

2 Hold the pieces together. Wrap tape around the two arms and the trunk of the slingshot to hold the pieces together.

3 Cut the rubber band. Poke one end through each hole of the slingshot. Tie each end to prevent the rubber band from slipping through.

1

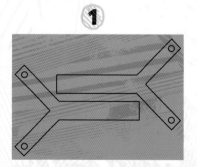

2

3

USING THE SLINGSHOT

1. Hold a foam ball against the rubber band, right in the middle.

2. Pull back, stretching the rubber band as far as you like.

3. Release the rubber band to send the foam ball on a wild ride!

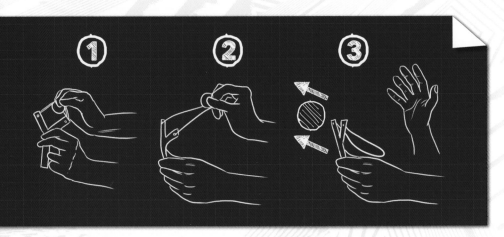

READY, AIM, SCIENCE!

Your slingshot looks very different from your catapult, but they both work on the same principle. You're stretching a rubber band, which gives it potential energy, and then holding it in place. When you stop holding the rubber band, the potential energy is released. The rubber band snaps forward and launches the foam ball.

HAND CANNON

Those ever-useful rubber bands are back again in this cool hand cannon.

WHAT YOU NEED

- Two toilet paper tubes
- Scissors
- Heavy-duty tape
- Four small paper clips
- Two rubber bands
- Foam ball from this kit

MAKE THE CANNON

1 Cut open one toilet paper tube lengthwise. Roll the tube so it is now slightly slimmer than the uncut tube. Tape along the tube's seam to hold this shape.

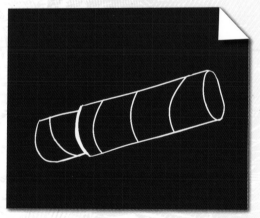

2 Completely cover one end of the cut tube with tape.

3 Insert the slim tube into the uncut tube.

4 Hook two paper clips to each rubber band.

5 Attach a paper clip from one rubber band to the open end of the smaller tube. Then stretch the rubber band to attach the other paper clip to the opposite end of the larger tube. Repeat this step with the other rubber band on the other side of the cannon.

6 Insert the foam ball into the open end of the cannon.

7 Hold the outer tube firmly and pull back on the inner tube. Release the tube and see the "cannonball" fly!

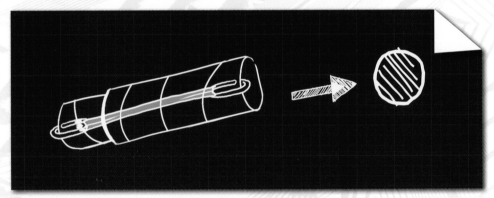

READY, AIM, SCIENCE!

It seems like there are infinite ways to use rubber bands to launch projectiles. The devices look different, but they all work on the same principle: the more you pull back on the rubber bands, the greater the stored energy and blasting power.

Would this hand cannon launch a NERF dart? Try it!

ARM POWER

In the previous activities, you created simple machines to launch projectiles. In this one, your body **IS** the machine. Use your arm and nothing else as a "blaster" to fire foam balls, marshmallows, tennis balls, or any other object. Just remember, never throw any objects at another person.

WHAT YOU NEED

- Foam ball in this kit, cotton balls, marshmallows, tennis balls, or any other nonbreakable objects you have at home

- Three objects to use as markers (such as rocks, sticks, or coins)
- A helper

GIVE US A HAND

 Make sure you have enough room to hurl your object.

 Your helper should move as far back from you as they think your object will land, making sure to look out for flying objects.

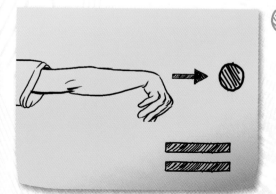

③ Throw your object at an angle that keeps it as parallel to the ground as possible. When it lands, have your helper mark the spot and run your object back to you.

4 Throw the same object again at an angle as close as possible to 45 degrees. Your helper should again mark the spot where your object lands and return the object to you.

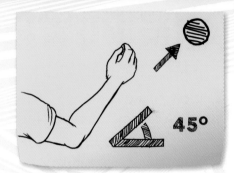

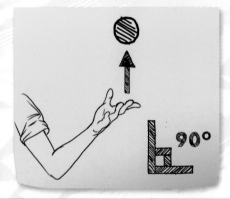

5 Throw the same object one last time at an angle as close as possible to 90 degrees. (Watch out!) Your helper should mark this spot, too.

READY, AIM, SCIENCE!

Your object—also known as a projectile—likely traveled farthest when you threw close to a 45-degree angle. When you throw your object at a smaller angle, the force of gravity and the fact that it is already so close to the ground make the object drop sooner.

When you throw your object at an angle close to 90 degrees, the force acting on the projectile is upward rather than forward. It will travel higher but fall sooner than a 45-degree-angle toss. Try this experiment with different types of projectiles and materials to see how your results vary.

TARGET SHOOTING

How's your aim? Test yourself and your friends to see who will be the Blast Master!

WHAT YOU NEED

- Large piece of paper
- Colored markers
- Tape
- Assortment of projectiles

BLAST AWAY!

1 On a large piece of paper, color a circular target. The target should have a big outer circle, then a medium circle, then a round bull's-eye in the middle.

2 Tape the target to a wall outdoors.

3 Take turns with your friends blasting projectiles at the target. Score one point for hitting the outer circle, two points for hitting the middle circle, and three points for hitting the bull's-eye, Who has the most points after ten turns? Crown that friend the winner!

READY, AIM, SCIENCE!

There are lots of scientific laws involved in hitting a target. You have to judge your projectile's speed and trajectory, along with other factors like wind and target distance. You might not be consciously thinking about these things, but your brain is calculating them nonetheless!

STOMP LAUNCHER

Rubber bands aren't the only way to power projectiles. Plain old air provides a good push, too. Check it out with this simple air-powered stomp launcher.

WHAT YOU NEED

- Empty juice pouch
- Bendy drinking straw
- Tape
- NERF dart

ASSEMBLE THE LAUNCHER

1 Remove the straw from an empty juice pouch. Poke a regular-size straw into the hole instead, leaving the bendy part outside. You can widen the hole a bit with some scissors, if necessary, to make the straw fit.

2 Put tape over the straw to hold it in place and seal the hole.

3 Outdoors, blow gently into the pouch through the straw to inflate it. **WEAR GLASSES TO PROTECT YOUR EYES**. Make sure any bystanders are standing back.

4 Set the pouch on the ground and angle the straw upward. Slide a NERF dart onto the straw.

5 Now **STOMP** on the juice pouch as hard as you can. Watch as the dart goes flying!

6 Now, try it again, but this time put the palm of your hand on the juice pouch. Push down quickly. What happens now?

 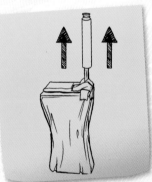

READY, AIM, SCIENCE!

When you stomp or press on the juice pouch, air squeezes out through the straw. Air exerts **PRESSURE** on objects. Ever been in a strong wind? Then you've felt a strong force! In this case, the blast of air hits the NERF dart, creating a wall of pressure that pushes the dart skyward. The harder you stomp, the more force there is and the farther the dart will go.

LUNG POWER

Besides a stomp launcher, do you know what else pushes air? Your lungs! Let's use some good old-fashioned lung power to launch a dart.

WHAT YOU NEED

- Shooter tube from this kit
- NERF dart

LUNG POWER!

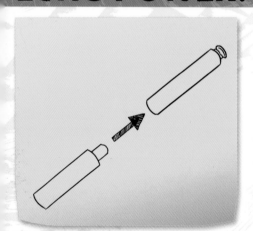

1. Insert the NERF dart into the tube.

2. Outdoors, put the tube's free end into your mouth and blow, blow, blow! How far can you launch the dart? It depends on your puffing power!

READY, AIM, SCIENCE!

Your lungs are big, spongy bags of air. When you exhale normally, air flows out without much force. If you want some extra push, muscles in your abdomen and between your ribs **CONTRACT** sharply to squeeze your lungs. The air is forced out quickly, pushing the dart as it goes. It's just like the juice pouch in the last activity, except inside your body.

WATER LAUNCH

Just like moving air, flowing water exerts force on objects. Does it push hard enough to launch a dart? Let's find out!

WHAT YOU NEED

- Shooter tube from this kit
- NERF dart
- Cup of water

LET'S GET WET!

1. Take all the components outdoors, because this is gonna get wet!

2. Take a big mouthful of water and hold it—don't swallow.

3. Put the dart onto one end of the shooter tube. Put the other end of the tube into your mouth.

4. Now blow, pushing the water into the tube. The water should come blasting out the other end, pushing the dart with it!

READY, AIM, SCIENCE!

Flowing water pushes against any objects it encounters. When you blow water into the shooter tube, you force the water out of the nozzle at high speed. The high-pressure water shoves against the dart and pushes it into flight.

PROJECTILES EVERYWHERE!

In this book, you have experimented with a few simple projectile devices. How does this apply to the real world? It turns out that projectiles are everywhere, and people have come up with some really cool ways to push them around. Check out these amazing examples.

AIRCRAFT CARRIERS

Aircraft carriers use steam-driven catapults to fling jets forward at high speed and help them take off in super-short distances. These catapults are so powerful, they can **ACCELERATE** a plane from 0 to 165 miles per hour (265 km/h) in two seconds!

SPACE SUITS

Astronauts can move around in space with the help of self-propelled suits. The suits are equipped with small nozzles that squirt out little blasts of nitrogen gas, which push the astronaut in the opposite direction. Here, the astronaut is the projectile!

VOLCANIC ROCKS

Rocks that blast out of volcanoes during eruptions are projectiles. They arc outward in a parabola, then plummet to Earth . . . hopefully not exactly where you're standing.

FIREWORKS

Fireworks are projectiles launched from tubes. At the bottom of the tube is an explosive powder. When the powder ignites, a chemical reaction occurs that makes gases expand rapidly. The expanding gases push the firework out of the tube at high speed. It rises up, up, up into the air before bursting.

MUSCLE POWER

Your muscles turn objects into projectiles all the time! When you throw or kick a ball, the ball is a projectile. When you push a door open or shut, the door is a projectile. You're giving these objects a little bit of your energy to make them move it, move it!

GLOSSARY

ACCELERATE: Increase in speed.

AIR RESISTANCE: The force that air exerts against a moving object.

CONTRACT: Get smaller by squeezing or forcing inward.

FORCE: Energy exerted on an object that can change the object's direction.

GRAVITY: A force that pulls objects toward the center of the Earth.

KINETIC ENERGY: Energy of an object in motion.

PARABOLA: The curved path of a projectile under the influence of gravity.

POTENTIAL ENERGY: Energy that is stored owing to an object's position or arrangement.

PRESSURE: Force spread out over an object.

PROJECTILE: Any object that moves through space or air and is subject only to gravity and, if there is any, air resistance.

TENSION: A pulling force exerted on a string, cable, or similar object.

THRUST: A pushing force that makes an object move forward.

TRAJECTORY: The path of a thrown object.